Love Letters to Jammie

Gertie Bates

MANIFOLD GRACE
Publishing House LLC

Published by Manifold Grace Publishing House, LLC.
Southfield, Michigan 48033
www.manifoldgracepublishinghouse.com

Dedication

I dedicate this book to my daughter, Aviance Patrice Darling.

She stays by my side during the hardest times of my life. She gave up so much of her life to look after me. She was my rock then, and she is my rock now.

Aviance, I want you to know I love you. Words can't explain the love I have for you. God gave you to me because He knew I needed you, and you would be there for me.

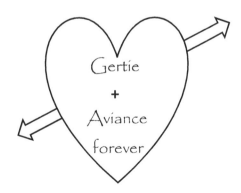

Acknowledgments

First, I want to thank God, without Him, I am nothing.

My two grandkids:
Chaise Aneres Darling
Ronald Douglass Darling III

My son, Giorgio Jamar Nealy

My brothers:
Norman Bates
Melvin Bates
Tommie Bates
Henry Bates
Leonard Tyrone White (deceased)

My sisters:
Carrie Bates (deceased)
Jacqueline Murriell

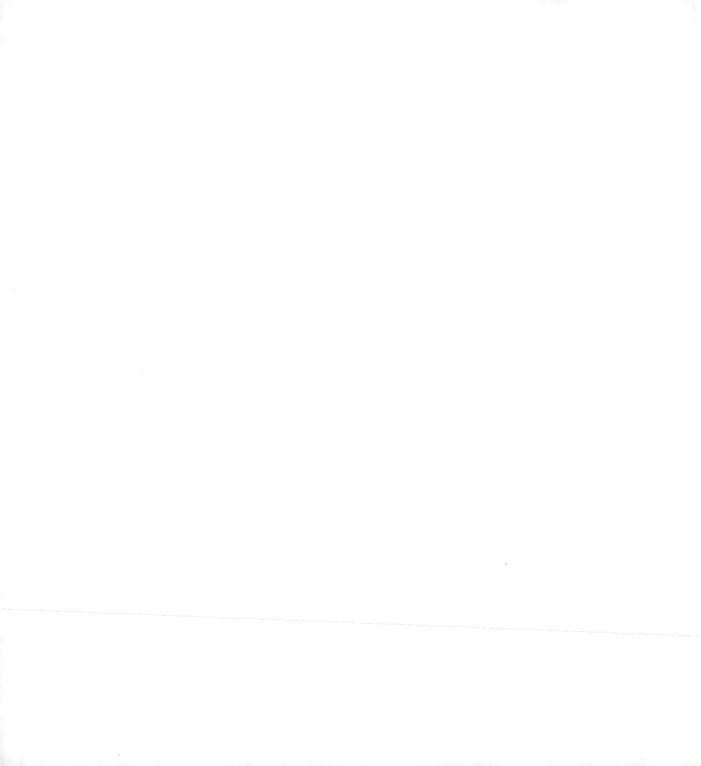

Introduction

The last years of my mother's life, I would say, took me to school. The school of my life, and what I was put here on earth to do. My mother was no longer teaching me as a child, but as the full-grown woman I was about to become. The most powerful knowledge of my life.

My daughter, my grandchildren and I love animals. I remember that my dog Spike used to trick my mother like he had to go potty. But he just wanted to go back outside. Mom taught us about animals.

I was with my mother from the beginning of my life, until the end of hers. That's why I can write and honor her in this book.

Thank you Mom.

"These arms around you, got you Gertie. I made you a promise the day you came into the world. I will never walk away from you; I will always love you.

"These arms are strong, that's the reason I put them around you when all hell is all around us. These arms will protect you."

Mom, you used to talk to me about peace. You would tell me it comes from inside. I did not understand then, but now I do. No person can give you this peace, it comes from God!

Look who's coming down the stairs. The woman, who, when I was a baby and I was crying, would pick me up. She would kiss me, rock me, and hold me to let me know everything was alright. I'm here forever, until death do us part.

You always dreamed big, even when you were a little girl. You would take nothing and make it into something. With just some simple bamboo mats, you took them and made them into a show piece that took everyone's breath away who came to our home.

You were always a very caring, friendly person. Your personality was out of this world! Psalm 23 was your favorite chapter in the Bible, now I understand why. *I will dwell in the house of the Lord forever.*

Mother, thank you for raising me in church and teaching me about God. Also, for telling me to never let go. Since you are not here anymore, I call on Him now. Mom you were right, God is bigger than you. I do remember what you used to tell me. God's love is unconditional and He will never leave you or forsake you. Believe, no matter what.

I love you Momma

Two hearts beat the same. All I know is, I feel love. I want to go wherever this lady goes. I have to be with her. I don't want to be without her. The big heart said, "I will be with you until the end of time."

Hey Jammie, who are you?

"The sun rose in my eyes on August 19, 1936. My name was Jammie Hansburg then. I was born in Midnight, Mississippi. I like the merchants ship that brought food from afar."

¹⁰Who can find a virtuous woman? for her price is far above rubies...²⁰She stretcheth out my hand to the poor; yea I reacheth forth my hands to the needy. ²¹ she not afraid of the snow for my household: for all my household are clothed with scarlet...²⁶She openeth my mouth with wisdom and in my tongue is the law of kindness...²⁸her children rise up and call me blessed. My husband also and he praiseth me. Proverbs 31:10-21,26,28.

Excerpt from Phenomenal Woman
by Maya Angelou

I walk into a room
Just as cool as you please,
And to a man,
The fellows stand or
Fall down on their knees.
Then they swarm around me,
A hive of honey bees.
I say,
It's the fire in my eyes,
And the flash of my teeth,
The swing in my waist,
And the joy in my feet.

I'm a woman
Phenomenally.

Now you understand
Just why my head's not bowed.
I don't shout or jump about
Or have to talk real loud.
When you see me passing,
It ought to make you proud.
I say,
It's in the click of my heels,
The bend of my hair,
the palm of my hand,
The need for my care.
'Cause I'm a woman
Phenomenally.

Phenomenal woman.

You go black Queen, walking the runway like a tall, proud woman who stands high, with that beautiful smile on your face. You say, "I'm here, after having 8 babies and working my fingers to the bone, taking care of them all."

I love you Momma

Mom, can you believe I have not been on a ship yet, at sea? I am afraid, just like you used to be, before you overcame your fear of the sea. I can't believe you did it. I want you to know I am very proud of you. You are a magnificent woman, and by the way, you look pretty. I love you always.

Mother, you are a leader of women and men; young and old. Women just wanted to get close to you, to touch your hand. Men wanted to talk to you and said, "Who is this woman that walks into the room and everything stops?"

"I'm here. Can you see me? I'm here, can you hear me? I'm here. Can you touch me? I'm here, I'm here." Yes Mom, I can see you, I can hear you and I can touch you. Yes Mom, I'm here, Gertie is here.

Little did I know Mom, 9 years after your death, you and my granddaughter would be singing the same song, your favorite. I had no clue the night me and Chaise started to practice this song. I found out when the song was done and out. Isn't it amazing I still think like you? You are not even here anymore.

I'm not surprised you are in God's house. That was your favorite place to be. Praying and begging God to always look after you and take care of your children.

Mom, I just want to tell you, you look so pretty going to church.

Mom, I'm happy you got a chance to enjoy some of your childhood dreams. You never gave up. You enjoyed every day of those childhood dreams that God allowed to come to pass. Every day was a new adventure. You lived life to the fullest.

I'm happy Mom. I gave you your flowers while you were here on earth, even though sometimes I acted up. I love you and miss you.

You don't know yet, but you are going to leave a legacy behind. Everybody is going to know the name, Jammie in Kalamazoo.

You are the prettiest woman I have ever seen in my life. Oh, I love that gold tooth in your mouth. How can a woman who had 8 children look like this? Mother, you used to always tell me, God kept you. Your skin, your hair, I love it.

I love you Mom

While we were both sitting there with our little smile. While love is powerful, I'm talking about the real love. The only love that comes after God's, is the love a mother gives her child. The love is so strong, we move our hands just alike. I know you got me Mom.

As I was sitting in your lap looking up into your eyes, I know I love you. You're looking down into my eyes saying *"I love you and I'm going to protect you and take care of you with every breath I've got."*

Hey Mom, when you passed away, the China Cabinet you gave me; Spike ran to it every day. He was barking, wagging his tail, jumping, looking at it - running around doing the same thing he used to do when you used to play with him. I know he sees an Angel, an Angel of you.

Mother, the way I love animals is because of you. I always watched the way you loved the animals, holding them, kissing them, making sure they were alright. You took care of me and my sister's dogs. You would drive 2 hours just to see them, buy their clothes and food.

Mom, you always taught us...

(1) Put God first

(2) Hard work, it does pay off

(3) Anything you want in life, don't ever stop

(4) Don't ever stop dreaming,

Look at you now, paid your own way to travel all over the world.
Oh yeah Mom, you look so beautiful.

I get it now Mom. Make a stand for what you believe in, because when you look back there's nothing there. Thank you.

I see the little girl that never got a chance to come out and play.
But now she's here. Have fun little girl, have fun.

With my big black curls touching the bottom of your face, you sat there thinking what to do next. Am I saying I got the best seat in the world, a seat that I'm not afraid of no matter how many times I fall off of it?

Mother, thank you for teaching me to keep going, even when I wanted to stop because I didn't see what I was looking for. Do what I have to do! Cry, kick, scream, yell, when I feel like God doesn't hear me. But after all that, get back up and start walking into my future without seeing it.

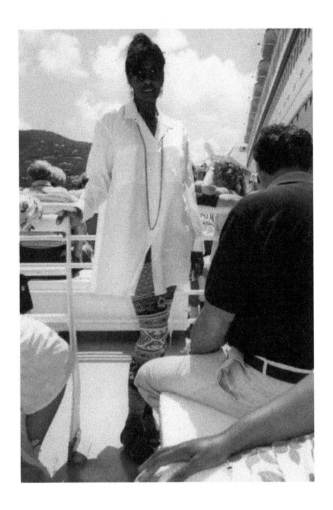

Wow, it's amazing. I'm looking at myself. I want to thank you Mom for allowing me to see what I'm going to look like when I get older.

You always lit up the room. Didn't matter where you were, what room you were in. God always had a light on you. Shining bright, with that beautiful smile and the personality that drew people to you.

Mom, you always had an eye for different and unique things, no matter where you were. You would find the things most people would dream about. You would put them together. It was a perfect match. Like the dress you have on and the big center piece, they go together. Good job Mom.

Mommy you always told us, "Do not be afraid to stand alone, as long as you put God first. Stand tall. Hold your head up high, because you are somebody."

Mom, you always told me a smile would go a long way. Even when I was sad and did not want to smile. But, little did you know that your smile would touch so many people with the word of God. Because, every person who was attracted to the smile, you told them about Jesus.

You have always been a thinker and very smart... before your time. You were a woman who came from the South with nothing. You worked your way up to have a good job. Took care of 8 children - even after we became grown; old enough even, to take care of ourselves. You always came to see about us, whatever problems we had. Didn't matter how far away we were, or what city we were in, you showed us you would give your life for us.

Even in your weakest days you still stood tall. *The Lord is my Shepherd I shall not want. He maketh me to lie down in green pastures: he leadeth me beside the still waters. He restoreth my soul: he leadeth me in the paths of righteousness for his name's sake. Yea though I walk through the valley of the shadow of death, I will fear no evil: for thou art with me: thy rod and thy staff they comfort me. Thou preparest a table before me in the presence of mine enemies: thou anointest my head with oil; my cup runneth over. Surely goodness and mercy shall follow me all the days of my life: and I will dwell in the house of the Lord forever.* Psalm 23

Mom, something I want to let you know. To me, you were the most powerful woman in the world. You had ten children – lost 2, took care of all your children. You started in the South with nothing. Not one day did we go hungry. Roof over our head, a place to live, shoes on our feet, clothes to wear. Did not matter if we had to wear hand me down clothes and shoes. You kept them washed and clean.

You were the one who went without and cried at night, but we could not see you. It was always another day for us because you kept going and going. You never gave up. The next day turned into years. The day you stopped was Sunday, November 13, 2011. You went to see our Lord and savior, Jesus Christ. I pray and hope I can be half the woman you were.

I love you Mother,

And I miss you!

My Love Letter to Jammie

First day I opened my eyes, there was you. First food into my body, there was you.

First word out of my mouth, there was you. First time I walked, there was you.

First time I rode a bike, there was you.

First time I went to school, there was you. My first fall, there was you.

First time I got my heart broken, there was you.

My first car, there was you.

My first major achievement, there was you. My first real love, was you.

My first real hurt and sorrow was the day you went away. I love you Mom, always.

Love, your daughter,
Gertie Bates

Author

I believe in love,

I believe God put us all on this earth to help each other.

I believe in helping animals that need help.

I believe in honoring your mother and father.

I believe, when you see another human being who might not look like you, or talk like you, their skin color might not be the same as yours – but if they need help, you should help them.

Anyone who does not love, does not know God, because God is love.   I John 4:8

I am Gertie Bates

I am the mother of one son, one daughter, one grandson and one granddaughter. I am a child of God. I am an author and manager of my granddaughter's singing career. I help my daughter as a stay at home teacher, for my grandchildren. It is one of the greatest accomplishments of my life.

I live in Westland, Michigan and am available for speaking engagements and book club discussions. Email me at gertiespike@yahoo.com for more information about this book.

CPSIA information can be obtained
at www.ICGtesting.com
Printed in the USA
LVHW070915131220
674062LV00014B/249

9 781937 400965